Hey Luke,

Well now you're 5 years old. And still "Mr. Personalty" I'm so blessed that I've been able to share all your Birthdays.

Luke, you bring excitement and a feeling of being young again to all of us.

What makes your Birthday so special isn't Cake & Ice Cream It's you!!!

Love & Prayers
Grandma Taylor

9/07

99 00 01 02 03 RDS 10 9 8 7 6 5 4 3 2 1

www.andrewsmcmeel.com

Library of Congress Cataloging-in-Publication Data
Hickerson, Robert.
    What little boys do-- / Robert Hickerson.
        p.   cm.
    ISBN 0-7407-0092-8 (hc.)
    1. Boys Portraits. 2. Portrait photography. I. Title.
    TR681.B6H53 1999
    779'.25'092--dc21   99-21528
                                                                              CIP

Design by Holly Camerlinck

ATTENTION: SCHOOLS AND BUSINESSES

Andrews McMeel books are available at quantity discounts with bulk purchase for educational, business, or sales promotional use. For information, please write to: Special Sales Department, Andrews McMeel Publishing, 4520 Main Street, Kansas City, Missouri 64111.

What Little Boys Do...

Robert Hickerson

Andrews McMeel
Publishing

Kansas City

Monkey around

Read a
magic book

Discover

Concentrate

Explore

Shift gears

Fall

Tolerate

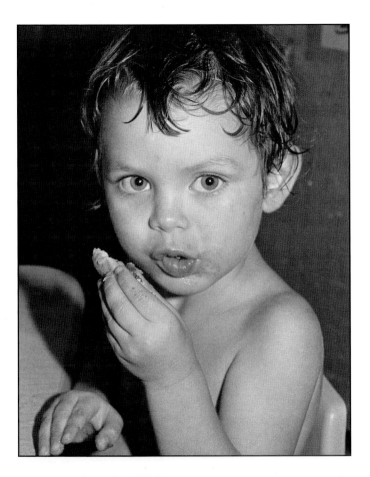

Tease

Snooze...

Eeeeehhh...

See
eye to eye

Savor

Hurry

Swing

Hot Doggin'

Housework

STRETCH

ANTICIPATe

Struggle

Hope